ED EMBERLEY'S DRAWING BOOK

MAKE A WORLD

LITTLE, BROWN
AND COMPANY
BOSTON—TORONTO

THIS BOOK WILL SHOW YOU
HOW TO DRAW ENOUGH THINGS
TO MAKE A WORLD OF YOUR OWN.

I HOPE YOU WILL TRY THIS WAY,
CONTINUE TO DRAW YOUR OWN WAY,
AND KEEP LOOKING FOR NEW WAYS—
I DO.

Happy Drawing!

Ed Emberley

ISBN 0-316-23598-9 (hc)
ISBN 0-316-23644-6 (pb)

Library of Congress Catalog Card Number 70-154962

HC: 20 19 18 17 16 15 14
PB: 10 9 8 7 6 5

BP

Published simultaneously in Canada by Little, Brown & Company (Canada) Limited

Printed in the United States of America

IF YOU CAN DRAW THESE THINGS ——→
YOU CAN DRAW ALL THE OBJECTS
IN THIS BOOK. FOR, INSTANCE:
YOU USE THESE   ▆ ▲ ▲ ‖ ‖ • |
TO MAKE THIS FISH   ><>
  THE DIAGRAMS ON THE
FOLLOWING PAGES WILL SHOW
    YOU HOW.

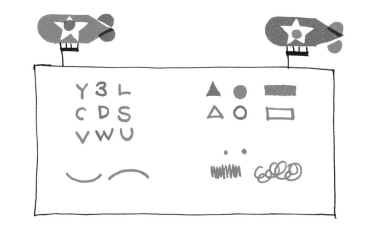

Y 3 L   ▲ ● ▬
C D S   △ ○ ▭
V W U

‿ ⌣   ⌇⌇ ⟲⟲

Other Books by Ed Emberley:

THE ARTWORK FOR THIS
BOOK WAS DRAWN ON
STRATHMORE PAPER
WITH FELT TIP AND
RAPIDOGRAPH PENS,
FOUR-COLOR, PRESEPARATED
AND HAND-LETTERED
BY THE AUTHOR.

CARS

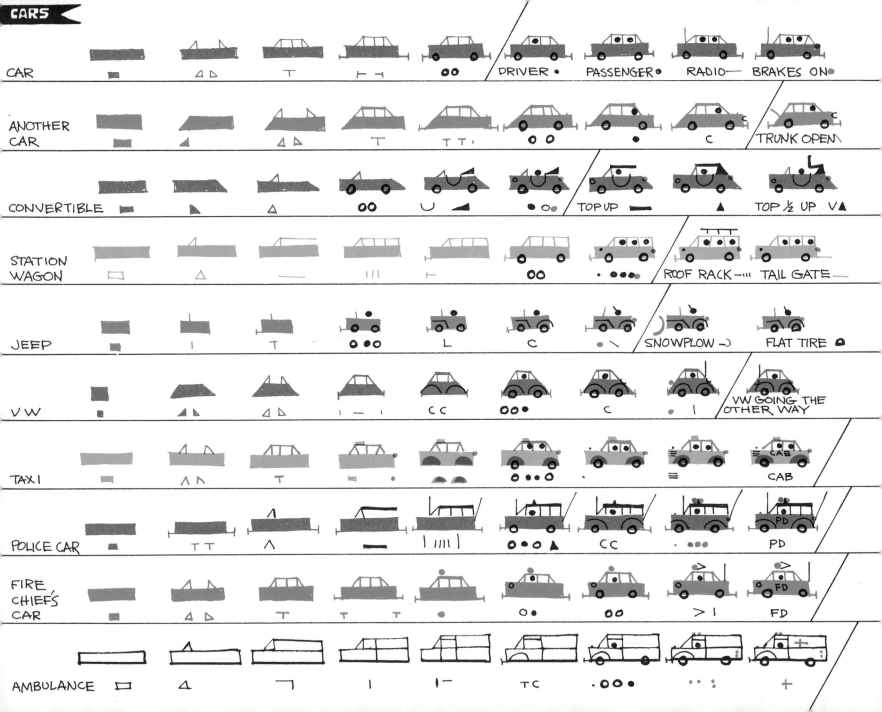

CAR						DRIVER •	PASSENGER •	RADIO —	BRAKES ON •
	▢	△ ▷	T	⊢ ⊣	OO				

ANOTHER CAR								C	TRUNK OPEN
	▭	◢	△ ▷	T	T T ˈ	O O	•	C	

CONVERTIBLE							TOP UP —	▲	TOP ½ UP V▲
	▭	◣	△	OO	∪ ◢	• O•			

STATION WAGON							ROOF RACK —ııı	TAIL GATE —
	▱	△	—	ııı	⊢	OO	• • • •		

JEEP							SNOWPLOW —)	FLAT TIRE ◖
	▭	ı	T	O O O	L	C	• \		

V W									VW GOING THE OTHER WAY
	▪	◢◣	△ ▷	ı — ı	C C	O O •	C	• ı	

TAXI							=	CAB
	▭	∧ ▷	T	•	O O • •	•	≡	CAB

POLICE CAR									
	▪	T T	∧	—	ı ıııı ı	O • O ◢	C C	• • •	PD

FIRE CHIEF'S CAR									
	▭	△ ▷	T	T T	•	O •	O O	> ı	FD

AMBULANCE									
	▱	△	⌐	ı	⊢	T C	• O O •	• • • •	+

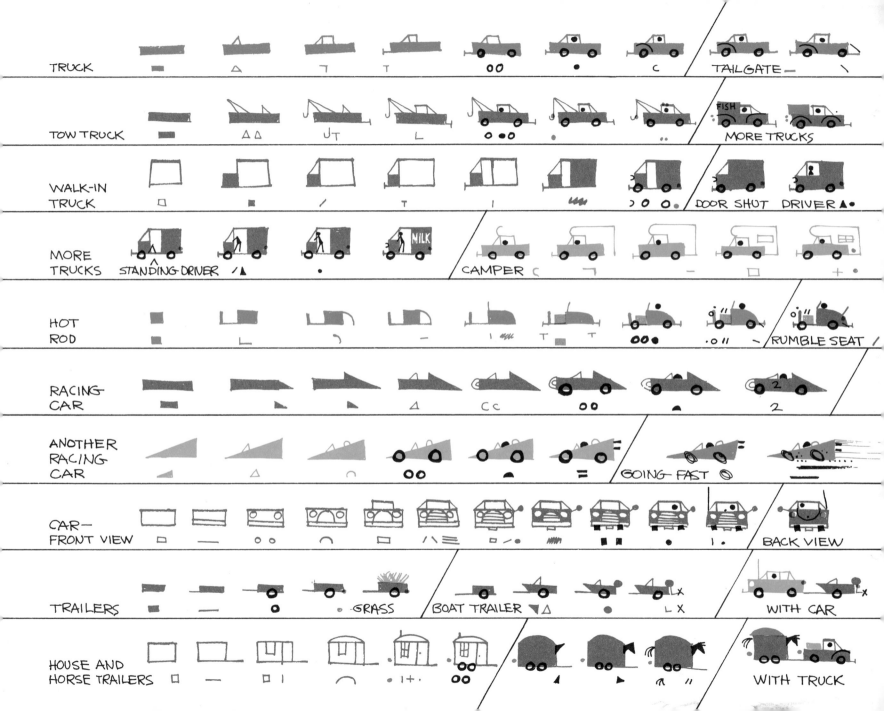

TRUCK · · △ · ⊓ · ⊤ · 00 · · C · TAILGATE —

TOW TRUCK · · △△ · ∪⊤ · L · 0 0 0 · · · · FISH · MORE TRUCKS

WALK-IN TRUCK · □ · ■ · / · ⊤ · I · ⌇ · > 0 0 · DOOR SHUT · DRIVER ▲ ·

MORE TRUCKS · STANDING DRIVER ∧ · /▲ · · · MILK · CAMPER C · ⌐ · — · □ · + ·

HOT ROD · ■ · L · ⌐ · — · I ⌇ · ⊤ ■ ⊤ · 00● · · 0II · — · RUMBLE SEAT /

RACING CAR · ▭ · ◢ · ◣ · △ · C C · 00 · ● · 2

ANOTHER RACING CAR · ◢ · △ · ⌒ · 00 · ● · = · GOING FAST ◎ ·

CAR—FRONT VIEW · □ · — · 0 0 · ⌒ · □ · ∧I≡ · ◻ / · ///// · ■■ · ● · I . · BACK VIEW

TRAILERS · ■ · — · ● · · GRASS · BOAT TRAILER ▽△ · ● · L X · WITH CAR X

HOUSE AND HORSE TRAILERS · □ · — · □I · ⌒ · · I+ · 00 · ◢ · ▶ · ⌢ · ◌ · WITH TRUCK

TRUCKS

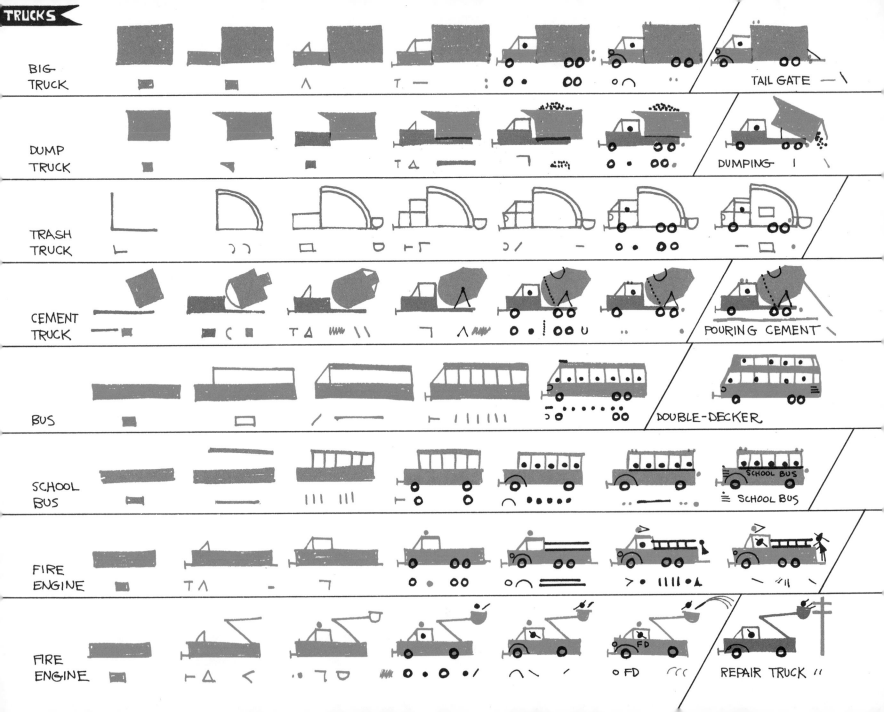

BIG TRUCK — TAIL GATE

DUMP TRUCK — DUMPING

TRASH TRUCK

CEMENT TRUCK — POURING CEMENT

BUS — DOUBLE-DECKER

SCHOOL BUS — SCHOOL BUS

FIRE ENGINE

FIRE ENGINE — REPAIR TRUCK

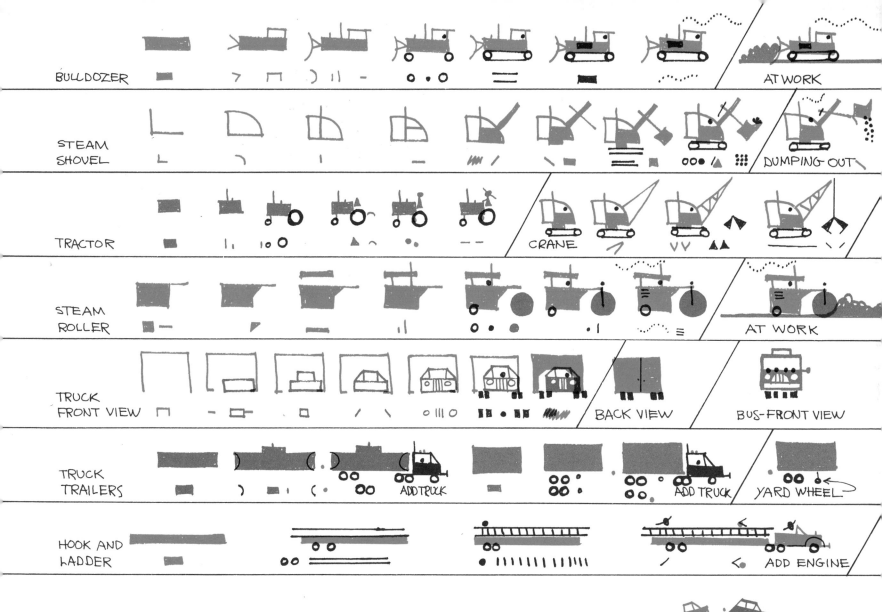

BULLDOZER ... **AT WORK**

STEAM SHOVEL ... **DUMPING OUT**

TRACTOR ... **CRANE**

STEAM ROLLER ... **AT WORK**

TRUCK FRONT VIEW ... **BACK VIEW** ... **BUS-FRONT VIEW**

TRUCK TRAILERS ... **ADD TRUCK** ... **ADD TRUCK** / **YARD WHEEL**

HOOK AND LADDER ... **ADD ENGINE**

CAR CARRIER ... **ADD CARS** ... **ADD CARS AND TRUCK**

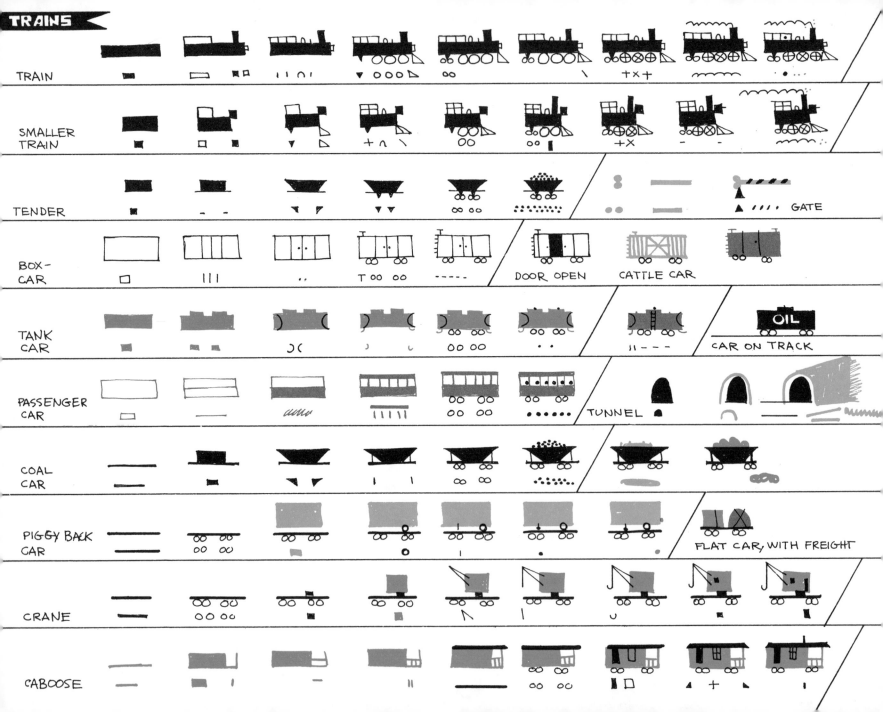

TRAINS

TRAIN

SMALLER TRAIN

TENDER ... GATE

BOX-CAR ... DOOR OPEN ... CATTLE CAR

TANK CAR ... CAR ON TRACK ... OIL

PASSENGER CAR ... TUNNEL

COAL CAR

PIGGY BACK CAR ... FLAT CAR, WITH FREIGHT

CRANE

CABOOSE

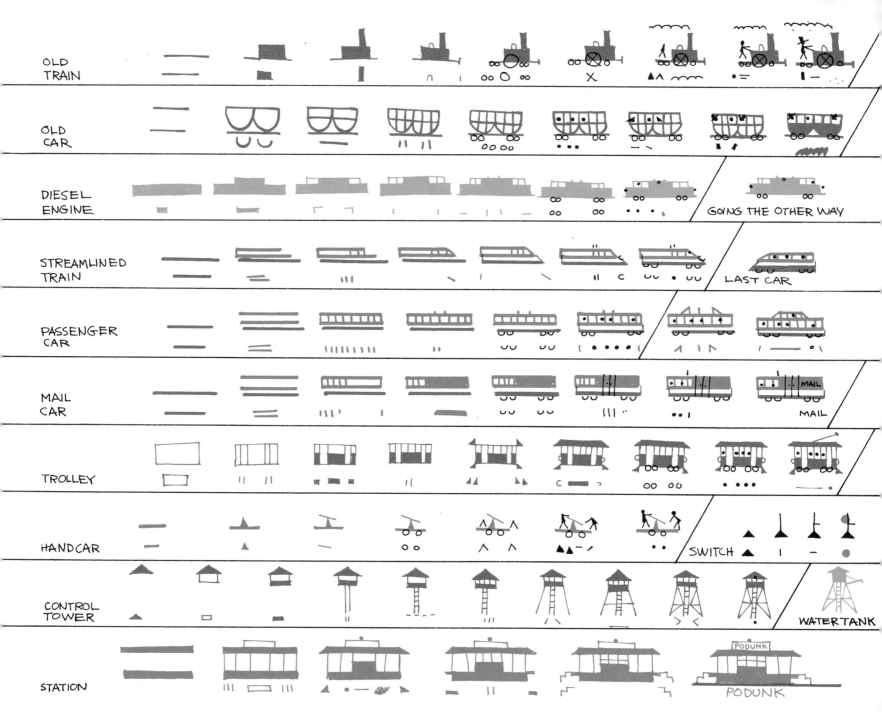

OLD TRAIN

OLD CAR

DIESEL ENGINE — GOING THE OTHER WAY

STREAMLINED TRAIN — LAST CAR

PASSENGER CAR

MAIL CAR — MAIL

TROLLEY

HANDCAR — SWITCH

CONTROL TOWER — WATERTANK

STATION — PODUNK

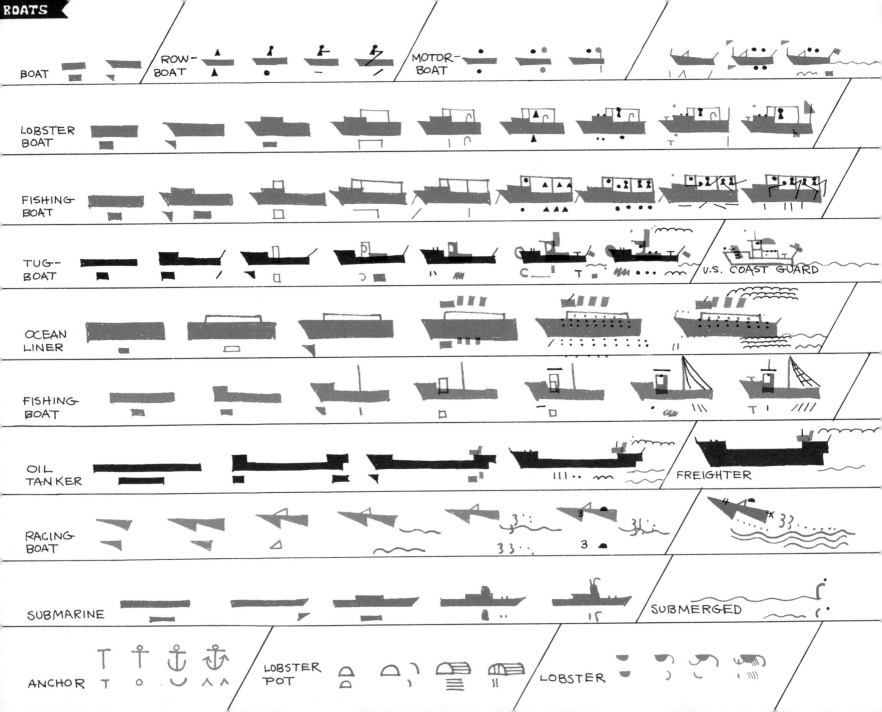

BOATS

BOAT

ROW-BOAT

MOTOR-BOAT

LOBSTER BOAT

FISHING BOAT

TUG-BOAT

U.S. COAST GUARD

OCEAN LINER

FISHING BOAT

OIL TANKER

FREIGHTER

RACING BOAT

SUBMARINE

SUBMERGED

ANCHOR

LOBSTER POT

LOBSTER

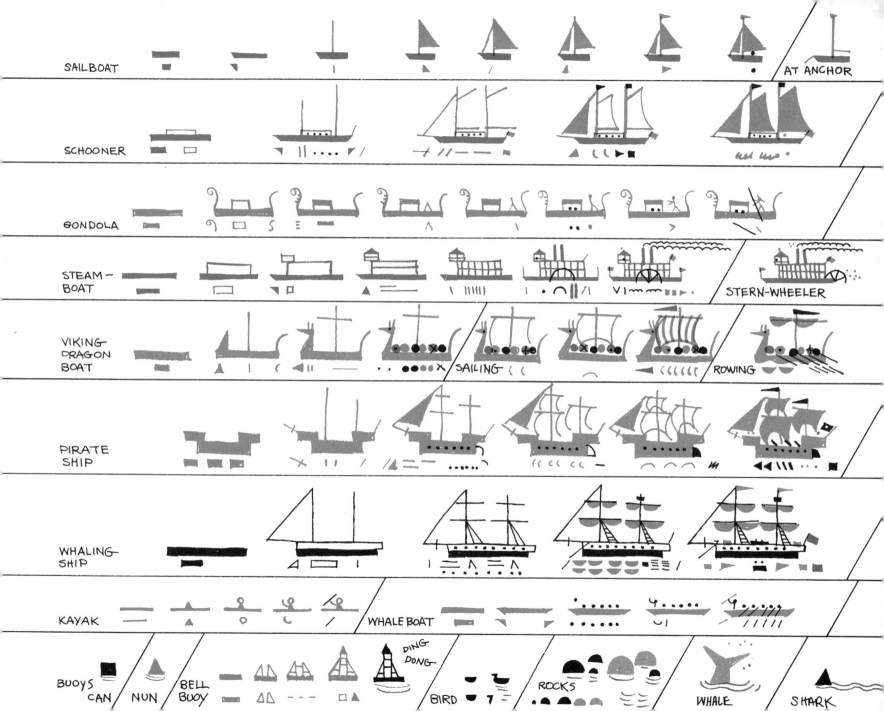

SAILBOAT
AT ANCHOR

SCHOONER

GONDOLA

STEAM-BOAT
STERN-WHEELER

VIKING DRAGON BOAT
SAILING
ROWING

PIRATE SHIP

WHALING SHIP

KAYAK
WHALE BOAT

BUOYS
CAN NUN BELL BUOY
DING DONG
BIRD ROCKS WHALE SHARK

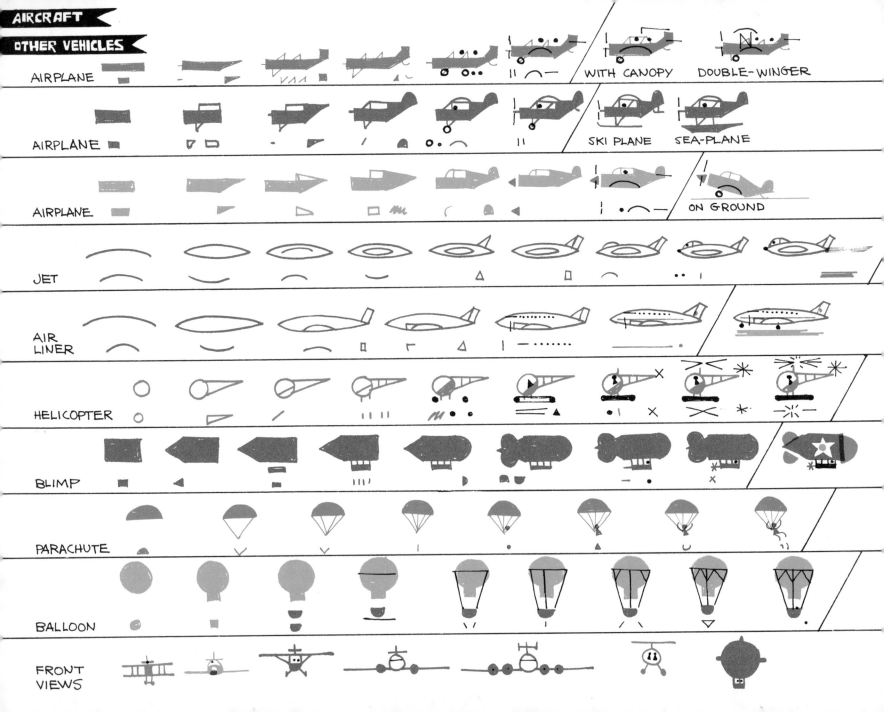

AIRCRAFT

OTHER VEHICLES

AIRPLANE

WITH CANOPY   DOUBLE-WINGER

AIRPLANE

SKI PLANE   SEA-PLANE

AIRPLANE

ON GROUND

JET

AIR
LINER

HELICOPTER

BLIMP

PARACHUTE

BALLOON

FRONT
VIEWS

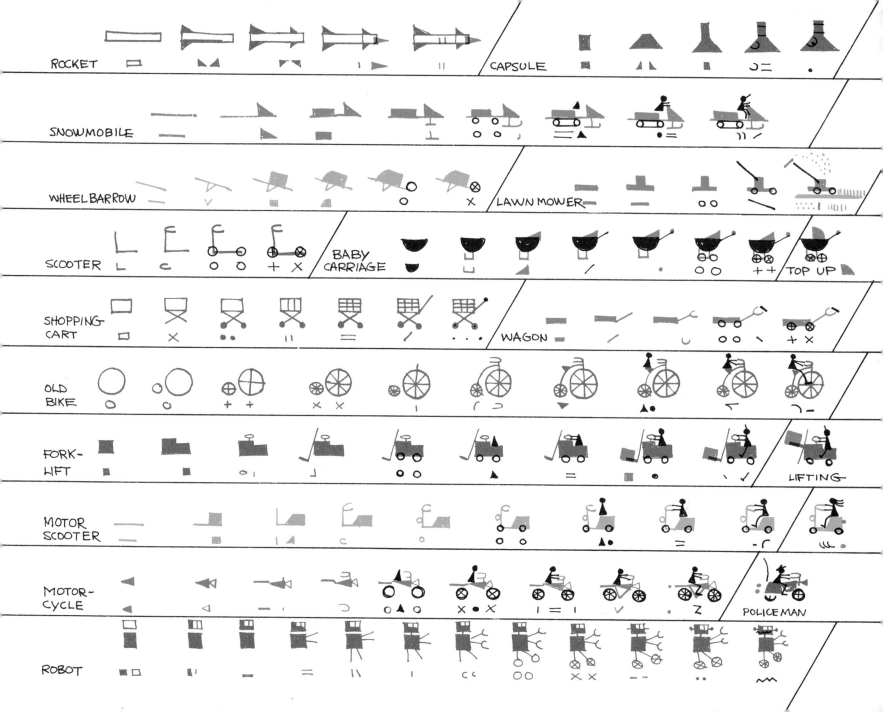

ROCKET

CAPSULE

SNOWMOBILE

WHEELBARROW

LAWN MOWER

SCOOTER

BABY CARRIAGE

TOP UP

SHOPPING CART

WAGON

OLD BIKE

FORK-LIFT

LIFTING

MOTOR SCOOTER

MOTOR-CYCLE

POLICEMAN

ROBOT

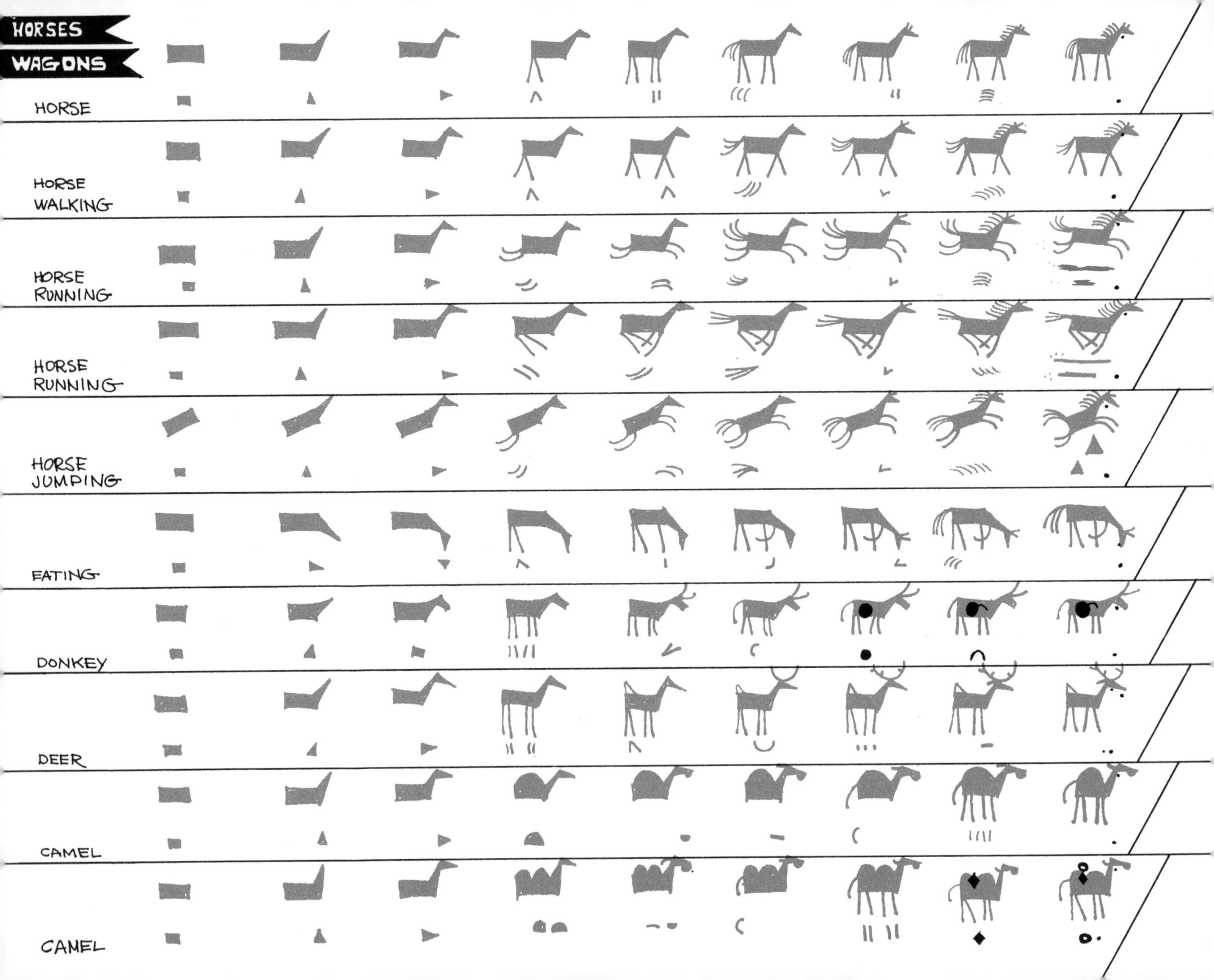

HORSE

HORSE
WALKING

HORSE
RUNNING

HORSE
RUNNING

HORSE
JUMPING

EATING

DONKEY

DEER

CAMEL

CAMEL

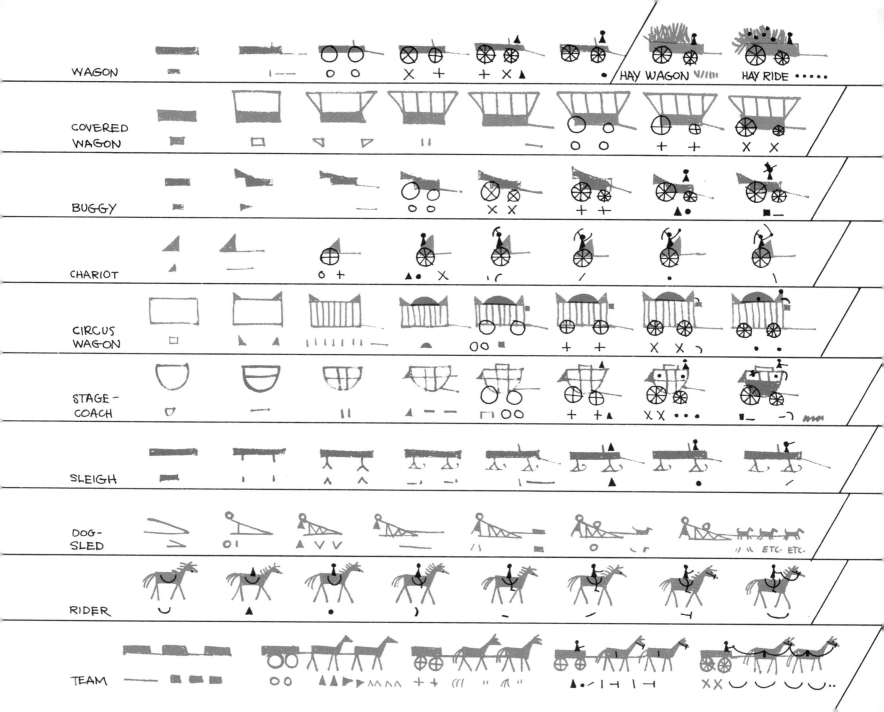

WAGON   HAY WAGON   HAY RIDE

COVERED WAGON

BUGGY

CHARIOT

CIRCUS WAGON

STAGE-COACH

SLEIGH

DOG-SLED   ETC. ETC.

RIDER

TEAM

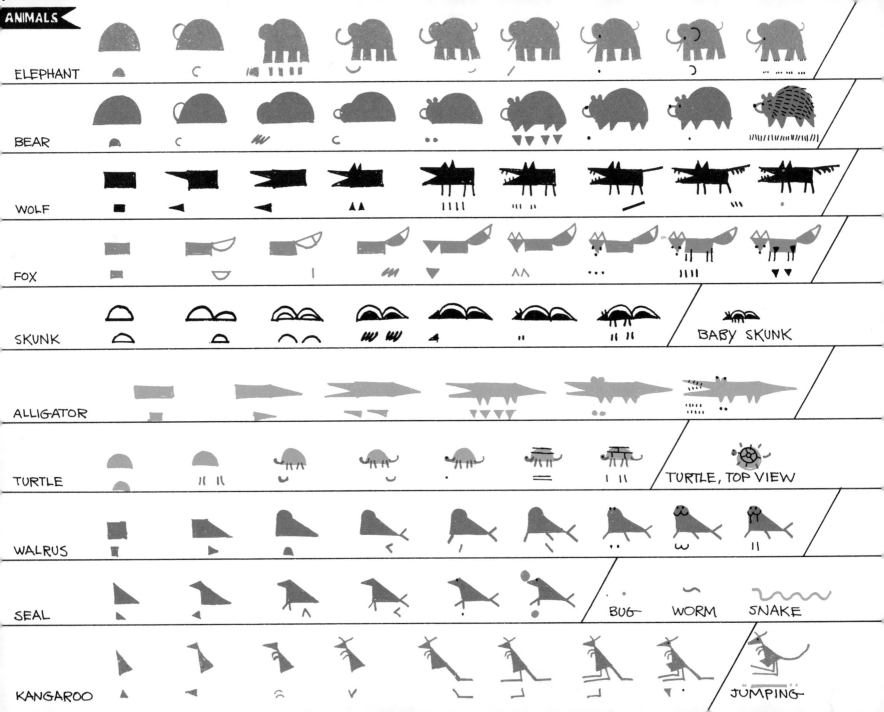

ANIMALS

ELEPHANT

BEAR

WOLF

FOX

SKUNK

BABY SKUNK

ALLIGATOR

TURTLE

TURTLE, TOP VIEW

WALRUS

SEAL

BUG   WORM   SNAKE

KANGAROO

JUMPING

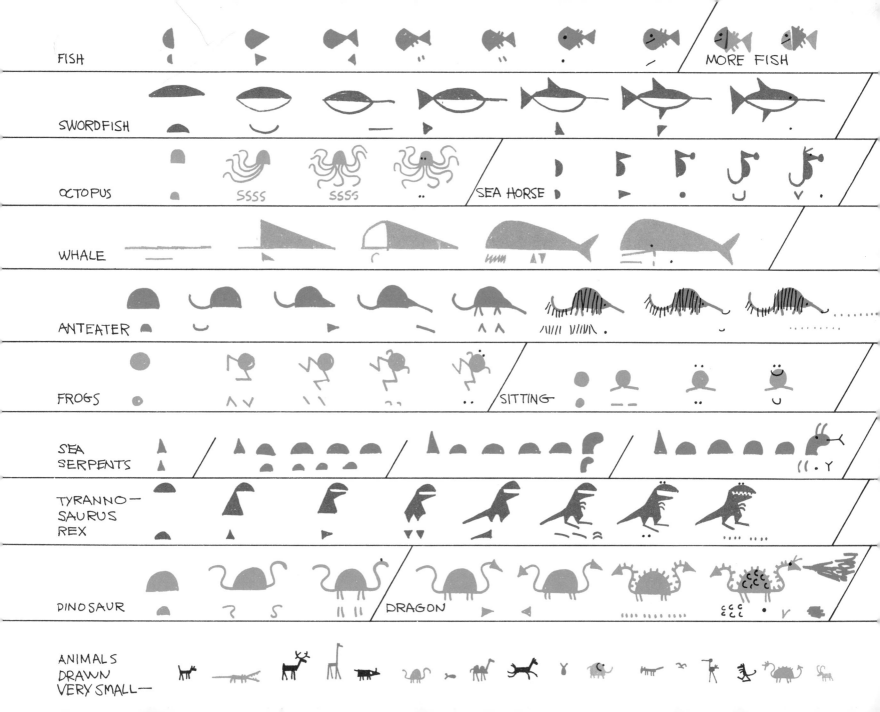

FISH

MORE FISH

SWORDFISH

OCTOPUS

SSSS SSSS

SEA HORSE

WHALE

ANTEATER

FROGS

SITTING

SEA
SERPENTS

TYRANNO-
SAURUS
REX

DINOSAUR

DRAGON

ANIMALS
DRAWN
VERY SMALL—

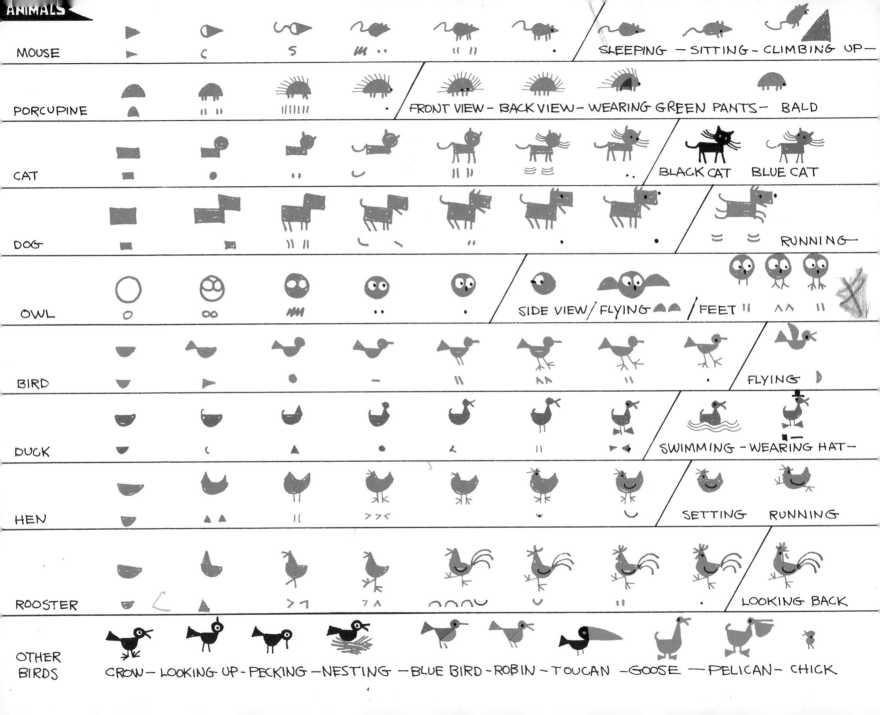

ANIMALS

| MOUSE | | | | | | | SLEEPING — SITTING — CLIMBING UP — |

| PORCUPINE | | | | FRONT VIEW — BACK VIEW — WEARING GREEN PANTS — BALD |

| CAT | | | | | | | | BLACK CAT   BLUE CAT |

| DOG | | | | | | | | RUNNING |

| OWL | | | | | | SIDE VIEW / FLYING / FEET |

| BIRD | | | | | | | | FLYING |

| DUCK | | | | | | | SWIMMING — WEARING HAT — |

| HEN | | | | | | | SETTING   RUNNING |

| ROOSTER | | | | | | | | LOOKING BACK |

| OTHER BIRDS | CROW — LOOKING UP — PECKING — NESTING — BLUE BIRD — ROBIN — TOUCAN — GOOSE — PELICAN — CHICK |

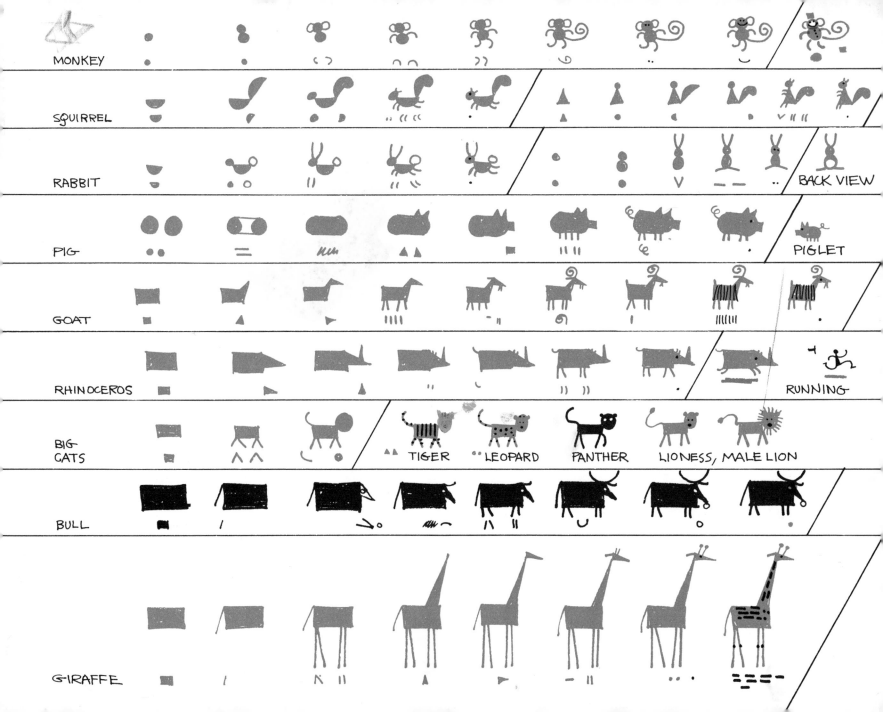

MONKEY

SQUIRREL

RABBIT   BACK VIEW

PIG   PIGLET

GOAT

RHINOCEROS   RUNNING

BIG CATS   TIGER   LEOPARD   PANTHER   LIONESS, MALE LION

BULL

GIRAFFE

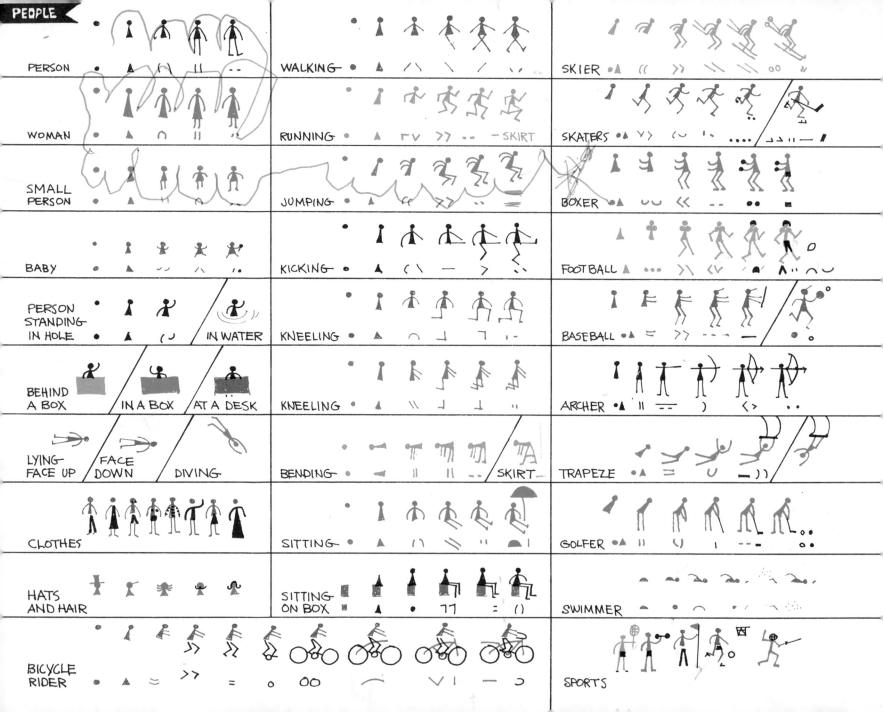

PEOPLE

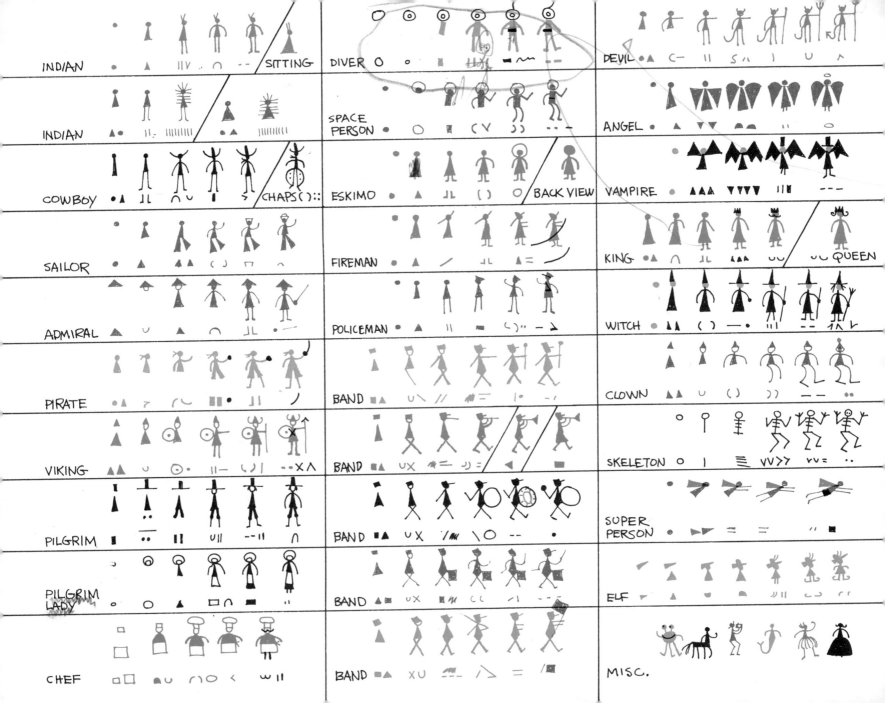

INDIAN

INDIAN

COWBOY

SAILOR

ADMIRAL

PIRATE

VIKING

PILGRIM

PILGRIM LADY

CHEF

SITTING

CHAPS

DIVER

SPACE PERSON

ESKIMO

FIREMAN

POLICEMAN

BAND

BAND

BAND

BAND

BAND

BAND

BACK VIEW

DEVIL

ANGEL

VAMPIRE

KING   QUEEN

WITCH

CLOWN

SKELETON

SUPER PERSON

ELF

MISC.

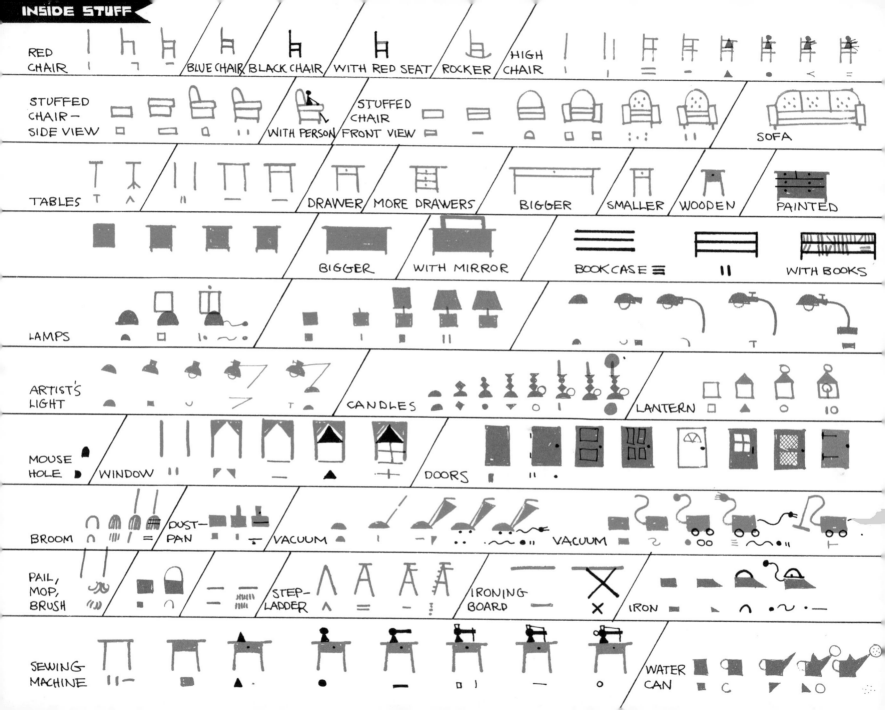

RED CHAIR

BLUE CHAIR BLACK CHAIR WITH RED SEAT ROCKER HIGH CHAIR

STUFFED CHAIR — SIDE VIEW

WITH PERSON STUFFED CHAIR FRONT VIEW

SOFA

TABLES

DRAWER MORE DRAWERS BIGGER SMALLER WOODEN PAINTED

BIGGER WITH MIRROR BOOKCASE WITH BOOKS

LAMPS

ARTIST'S LIGHT

CANDLES LANTERN

MOUSE HOLE WINDOW DOORS

BROOM DUST-PAN VACUUM VACUUM

PAIL, MOP, BRUSH STEP-LADDER IRONING BOARD IRON

SEWING MACHINE WATER CAN

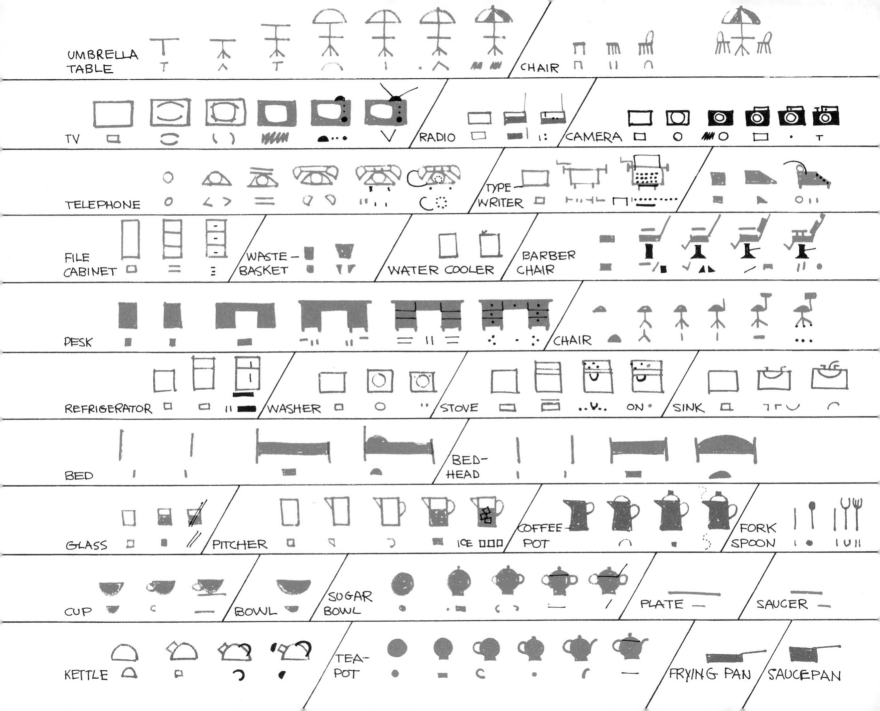

UMBRELLA TABLE

CHAIR

TV

RADIO

CAMERA

TELEPHONE

TYPE WRITER

FILE CABINET

WASTE-BASKET

WATER COOLER

BARBER CHAIR

DESK

CHAIR

REFRIGERATOR

WASHER

STOVE

ON

SINK

BED

BED-HEAD

GLASS

PITCHER

ICE

COFFEE-POT

FORK SPOON

CUP

BOWL

SUGAR BOWL

PLATE

SAUCER

KETTLE

TEA-POT

FRYING PAN

SAUCEPAN

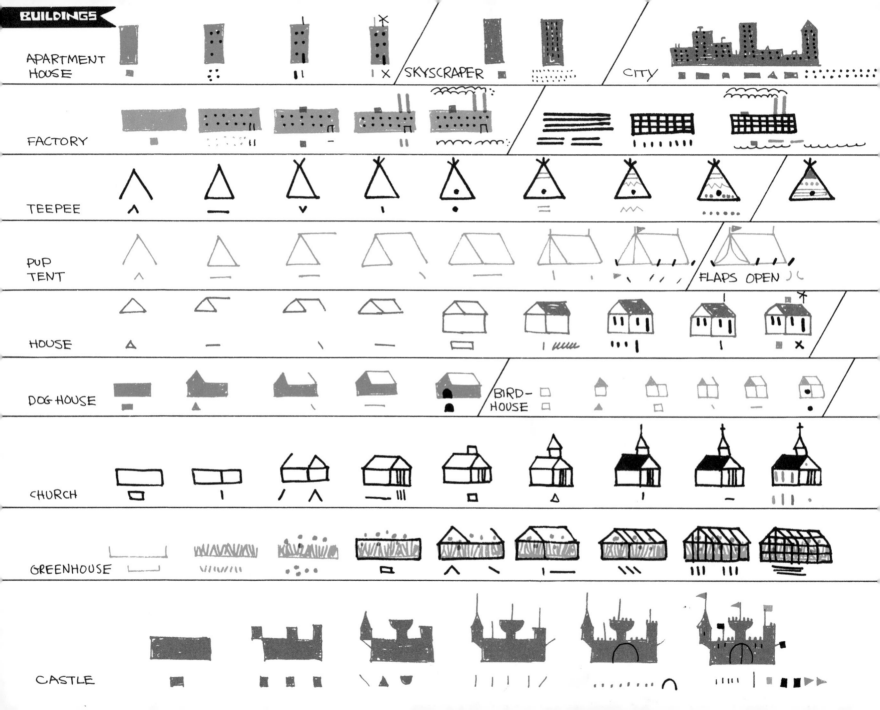

BUILDINGS

APARTMENT HOUSE

SKYSCRAPER

CITY

FACTORY

TEEPEE

PUP TENT

FLAPS OPEN

HOUSE

DOG HOUSE

BIRD-HOUSE

CHURCH

GREENHOUSE

CASTLE

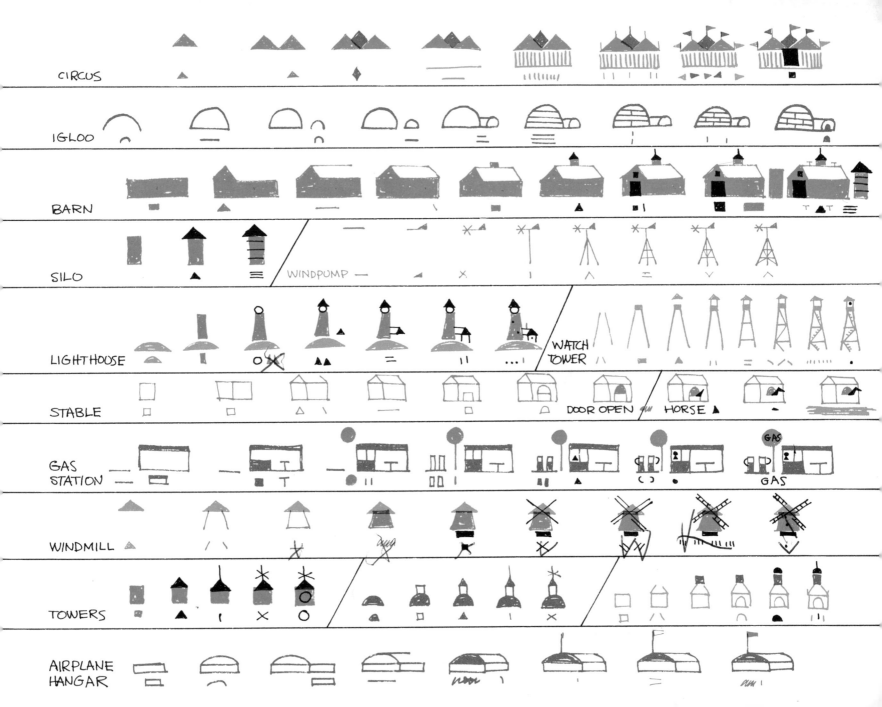

CIRCUS

IGLOO

BARN

SILO   WINDPUMP

LIGHTHOUSE   WATCH TOWER

STABLE   DOOR OPEN   HORSE

GAS STATION   GAS   GAS

WINDMILL

TOWERS

AIRPLANE HANGAR

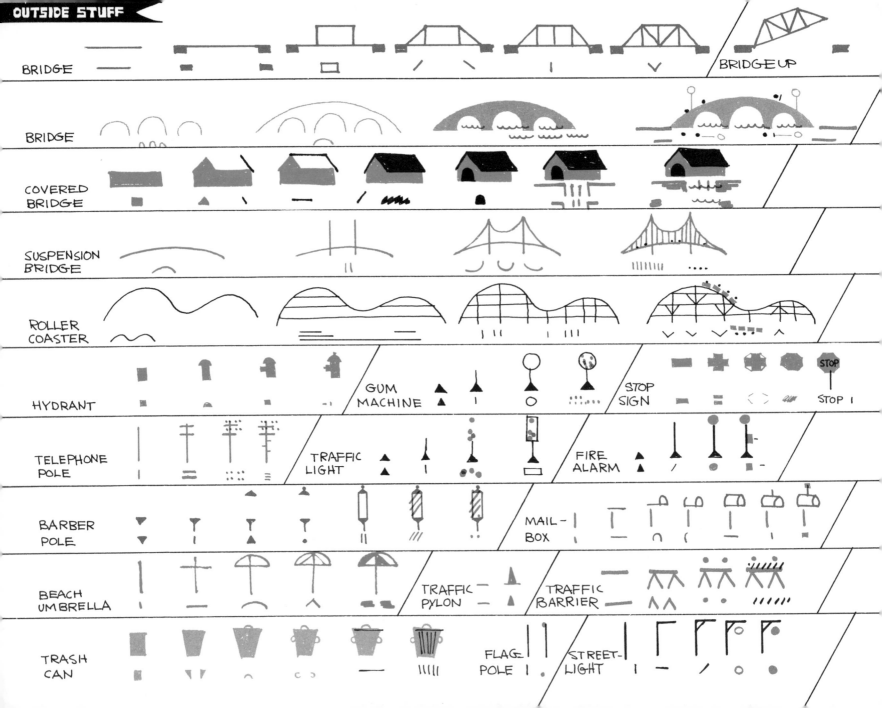

BRIDGE

BRIDGE UP

BRIDGE

COVERED BRIDGE

SUSPENSION BRIDGE

ROLLER COASTER

HYDRANT

GUM MACHINE

STOP SIGN

STOP

TELEPHONE POLE

TRAFFIC LIGHT

FIRE ALARM

BARBER POLE

MAIL-BOX

BEACH UMBRELLA

TRAFFIC PYLON

TRAFFIC BARRIER

TRASH CAN

FLAG POLE

STREET-LIGHT

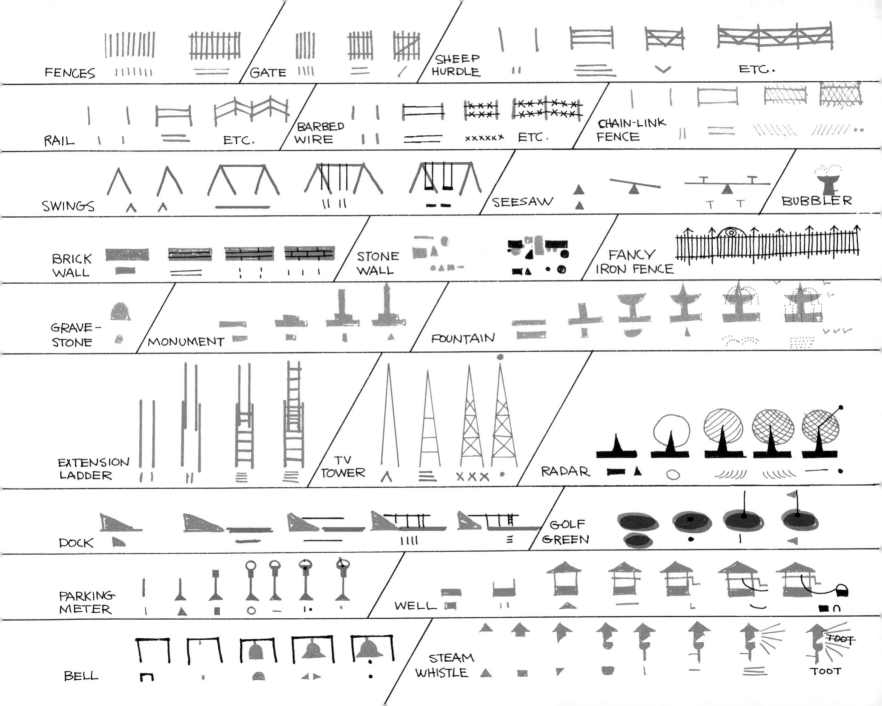

FENCES GATE SHEEP HURDLE ETC.

RAIL ETC. BARBED WIRE ETC. CHAIN-LINK FENCE

SWINGS SEESAW BUBBLER

BRICK WALL STONE WALL FANCY IRON FENCE

GRAVE-STONE MONUMENT FOUNTAIN

EXTENSION LADDER TV TOWER RADAR

DOCK GOLF GREEN

PARKING METER WELL

BELL STEAM WHISTLE TOOT TOOT

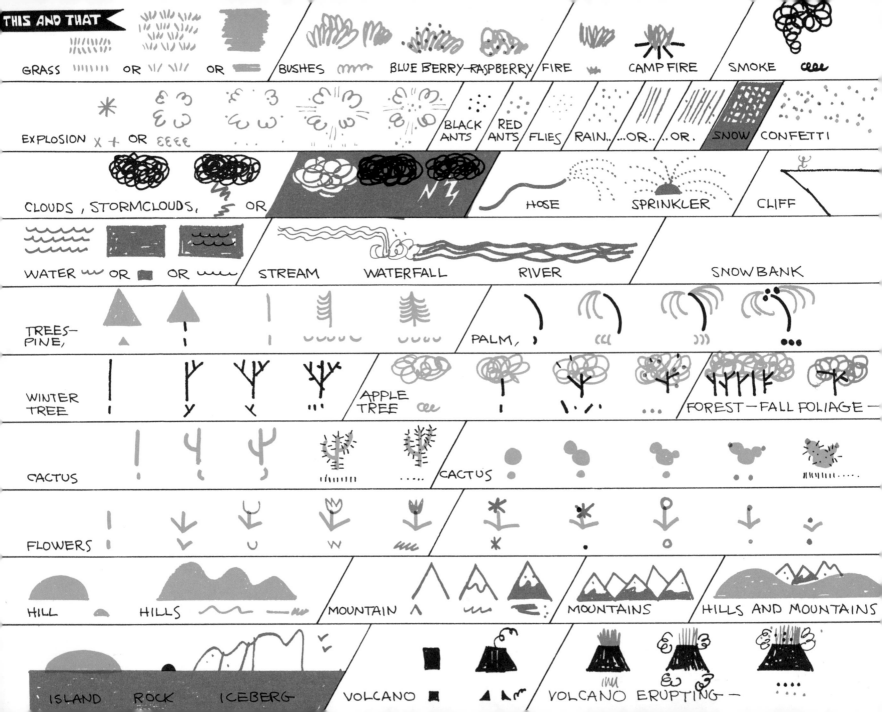

THIS AND THAT

GRASS OR OR BUSHES BLUE BERRY RASPBERRY FIRE CAMP FIRE SMOKE

EXPLOSION X + OR εεεε BLACK ANTS RED ANTS FLIES RAIN.. ..OR.. ..OR. SNOW CONFETTI

CLOUDS, STORMCLOUDS, OR HOSE SPRINKLER CLIFF

WATER OR OR STREAM WATERFALL RIVER SNOW BANK

TREES— PINE, PALM,

WINTER TREE APPLE TREE FOREST—FALL FOLIAGE—

CACTUS CACTUS

FLOWERS

HILL HILLS MOUNTAIN Λ MOUNTAINS HILLS AND MOUNTAINS

ISLAND ROCK ICEBERG VOLCANO VOLCANO ERUPTING—

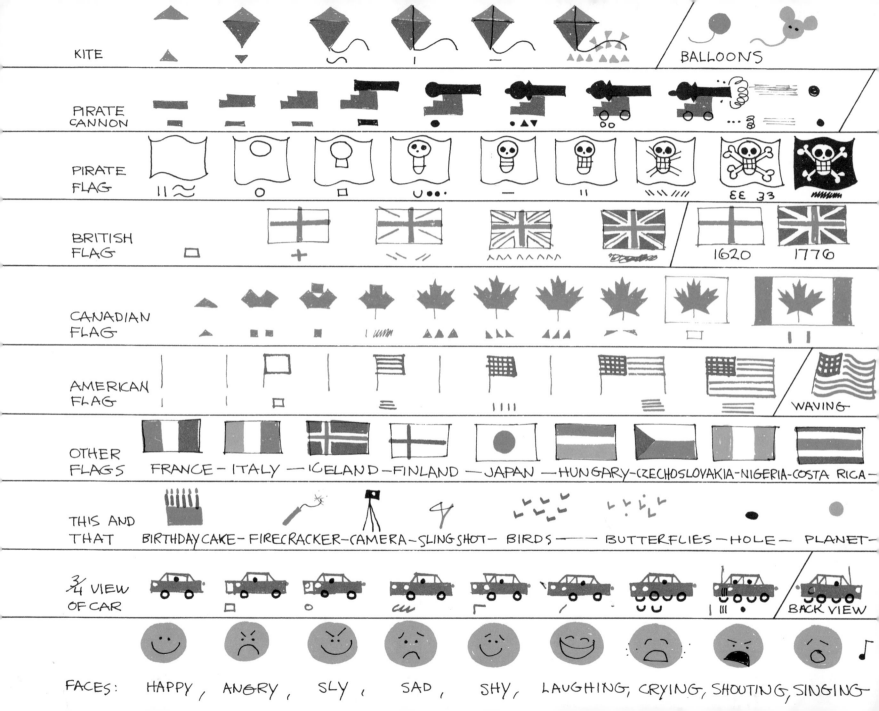

KITE

BALLOONS

PIRATE CANNON

PIRATE FLAG

BRITISH FLAG — 1620 — 1776

CANADIAN FLAG

AMERICAN FLAG — WAVING

OTHER FLAGS — FRANCE — ITALY — ICELAND — FINLAND — JAPAN — HUNGARY — CZECHOSLOVAKIA — NIGERIA — COSTA RICA —

THIS AND THAT — BIRTHDAY CAKE — FIRECRACKER — CAMERA — SLING SHOT — BIRDS — BUTTERFLIES — HOLE — PLANET —

¾ VIEW OF CAR — BACK VIEW

FACES: HAPPY, ANGRY, SLY, SAD, SHY, LAUGHING, CRYING, SHOUTING, SINGING

✳ HERE ARE SOME OF THE THINGS
YOU CAN DO WITH YOUR PICTURES...

COMIC STRIPS...

POSTERS...   PATTERNS...   BORDERS...

BOOKS....

GOOD KNIGHT

ONCE UPON A TIME...

THERE WAS A GOOD KNIGHT.

HE FOUGHT THE DRAGON

AND THEY LIVED

HAPPILY EVER AFTER.

MOBILES...

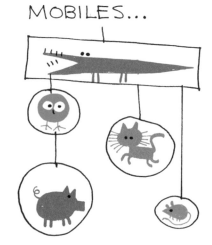

SIGNS...

KEEP OUT

WELCOME

CARDS...

BON VOYAGE

GREETINGS

LETTERS...

DEER ANNE:

HAVING FUN AT CAMP—

WISH YOU WERE HERE.

SUE

GAMES, ETC...

PIN THE TAIL ON THE DRAGON

THERE ARE MANY WAYS
THE DRAWINGS IN THIS BOOK AND YOUR OWN DRAWINGS
CAN BE PUT TOGETHER, ADDED TO OR CHANGED
TO MAKE SOME WORLDS OF YOUR OWN.
FOR INSTANCE...